Text by John Grenham
Heraldic Artwork by Myra Maguire
Featuring the photography of Michael Diggin

This edition published in 2005 by John Hinde

ISBN 0 7858 0083 2

THE LITTLE BOOK OF

IRISH CLANS

BY

JOHN GRENHAM

Published by
**John Hinde Ltd.,
Dublin, Ireland.**

INTRODUCTION

The history of Ireland is a great drama of war, invasion, plantation, immigration, emigration, conflict and solidarity. Like all history, however, it is composed of countless individual family histories, each unique. Surnames are the point where history and family history intersect, marking individuality and kinship.

The intermingling of cultures in Ireland – Gaelic, Viking, Norman, British – has created a huge number of surnames and left ambiguity surrounding the origins of many of them, an ambiguity that is itself a feature of Irishness. No description of Irish families and their surnames can afford to ignore this by selecting only those that match the history of one part of the population or one part of the island.

What follows is an account of some of the most common surnames in Ireland today, chosen purely because they *are* some of the most common, and therefore including some which are more usually seen as English or Scottish. Any surname, borne by an Irish person, whatever its origin, is an Irish surname.

Facing page: the Caragh River, near Glenbeigh
in Co. Kerry.

AHERNE

Aherne is an anglicisation of *Ó hEachthianna*, from *Eachthiarna,* meaning 'lord of horses', and is also found in the variants 'Hearn' and 'Hearne'. *Eachthiarna* was a relatively common personal name in Gaelic society, borne by, for instance, a brother of Brian Boru. The surname originated, in fact, in the sept or tribe of Brian, the *Dál gCais*, and has always been strongly associated with their homeland in Co. Clare. The family territory was in the southeast of the county, around Sixmilebridge, up to the end of the Middle Ages, when they migrated south and east, to counties Cork, Limerick and Waterford. To this day, Ahernes are most numerous in counties Cork and Waterford.

The arms of the family include three herons, in an obvious pun on the name.

BARRETT

The name Barrett is now concentrated in two widely separated parts of Ireland, in Co. Cork and in the Mayo-Galway region. The Irish version of the name is *Baróid* in the south and *Bairéid* in the west, and this may reflect two separate origins. At any rate, families of the surname first appeared in these areas in the thirteenth century, after the Anglo-Norman invasion. Its Norman origin derives it from the old Germanic personal name, Bernard or Beraud. A separate derivation gives its origin as the Middle English 'Barat', a nickname for a quarrelsome or deceitful person.

The western family, originally based around Killala in Mayo, were absorbed into Gaelic society very quickly, and in the Middle Ages began to split into various sub-clans, among them McAndrew, Timmons, and Roberts. The Cork settlers were not so Gaelicised, giving their name to the large barony of Barretts in the middle of the county.

BARRY

The first bearer of the surname to arrive in Ireland was Robert de Barri, one of the original band of Norman knights who landed at Bannow in Co. Wexford in May 1169, and a brother of Giraldus Cambrensis, historian of the invasion. The name comes from the earlier association of the family with the island of Barry, seven miles southwest of Cardiff in Wales. From the start the family were prominent in the settlement of east Cork, and were soon absorbed into the native culture, forming subsepts on Gaelic lines, the most important being Barry Mór, Barry Óg and Barry Roe. The names of two of these are perpetuated in the names of the Cork baronies of Barrymore and Barryroe, and many other Cork place names are linked to the family: Kilbarry, Rathbarry and Buttevant (from the family motto *Boutez en avant*), to mention only three. The surname is now numerous in Ireland, but still inextricably associated with Co. Cork.

BOYLE

Boyle, or O'Boyle, is now one of the fifty most common surnames in Ireland. In Irish the name is *Ó Baoghill*, thought to be connected to the Irish *geall*, meaning 'pledge'. In the Middle Ages the family were powerful, sharing control of the entire northwest of the island with the O'Donnells and the O'Dohertys, and the strongest association of the family is still with Co. Donegal, where (O)Boyle is the third most numerous name in the county.

The majority of those bearing the name are of Gaelic origin, but many Irish Boyles have separate, Norman origins. In Ulster, a significant number are descended from the Scottish Norman family of de Boyville, whose name comes from the town Beauville in Normandy. The most famous Irish family of the surname were the Boyles, Earls of Cork and Shannon, descended from Richard Boyle, who arrived in Ireland from Kent in 1588.

BRADY

The surname derives from the Irish *Mac Brádaigh*, coming, possibly, from *brádach*, meaning 'thieving' or 'dishonest'. The name remains very numerous in Co. Cavan, their original homeland, with large numbers also to be found in the adjoining county of Monaghan. Their power was centred on an area a few miles east of Cavan town, from where they held jurisdiction over a large territory within the old Gaelic kingdom of Breifne. There have been many notable poets, clergymen and soldiers of the name, including Thomas Brady (1752-1827), a field marshal in the Austrian army, the satirical Gaelic poet Rev. Philip MacBrady, as well as three MacBrady Bishops of Kilmore, and one MacBrady Bishop of Ardagh. The pre-Reformation Cavan Crozier, originally belonging to one of these MacBradys, is now to be found in the National Museum in Dublin.

BRENNAN

This is one of the most frequent surnames in Ireland. It derives from the two Irish originals *Ó Braonáin* and *Mac Branáin* . The *Mac Branáin* were chiefs of a large territory in the east of the present Co. Roscommon, and the majority of the Brennans of north Connacht, counties Mayo, Sligo and Roscommon, descend from them. *Ó Braonáin* originated in at least four distinct areas: Kilkenny, east Galway, Westmeath and Kerry. Of these the most powerful were the *Ó Braonáin* of Kilkenny, chiefs of Idough in the north of the county. After they lost their land to the English, many of them became notorious as leaders of outlaw bands.

A separate family, the *Ó Branáin*, are the ancestors of many of the Brennans of counties Fermanagh and Monaghan, where the name was also anglicised as Brannan and Branny.

BROWNE

This is one of the most common surnames in the British Isles, and is among the forty commonest in Ireland. It can derive, as a nickname, from the Old English *Brun*, referring to hair, complexion or clothes, or from the Norman name *Le Brun*, similarly meaning 'the Brown'. In the three southern provinces of Munster, Leinster and Connacht, where the name is usually spelt with the final 'e', it is almost invariably of Norman or English origin, and was borne by some of the most important of Norman-Irish and Anglo-Irish families, notably the Earls of Kenmare in Kerry and Lord Oranmore and Browne and the Earls of Altamont in Connacht.

In Ulster, where it is more often plain 'Brown', the surname can be an anglicisation of the Scots Gaelic *Mac a' Bhruithin* ('son of the judge') or *Mac Gille Dhuinn* ('son of the brown boy').

BURKE

Burke, along with its variants Bourke and de Burgh, is the most common Irish name of Norman origin; over 20,000 Irish people bear the surname.

The first person of the name to arrive in Ireland was William Fitzadelm de Burgo, a Norman knight from Burgh in Suffolk, who took part in the invasion of 1171 and succeeded Strongbow as Chief Governor. He received the earldom of Ulster, and was granted territory in Connacht. His descendants adopted Gaelic laws and customs more completely than any of the other Norman invaders, and quickly became one of the most important families in the country.

According to legend, the arms of the family originated during the Crusades, when King Richard dipped his finger in the blood of a Saracen slain by one of the de Burghs, drew a cross on the Saracen's golden shield, and presented it to the victor.

BUTLER

The surname Butler is Norman in origin, and once meant 'wine steward'. The name was then extended to denote the chief servant of a household and, amongst the nobility, a high-ranking officer concerned only nominally with the supply of wine.

In Ireland the most prominent Butler family is descended from Theobald Fitzwalter, who was created 'Chief Butler' of Ireland by Henry II. His descendants became the Earls and later the Dukes of Ormond. Up to the end of the seventeenth century, the Butlers were one of the most powerful Anglo-Norman dynasties, sharing effective control of Ireland with their great rivals the Fitzgeralds.

Kilkenny Castle, from 1391 until 1936 the chief seat of the Butler earls and dukes of Ormond.

BYRNE

Byrne or O'Byrne, together with its variants Be(i)rne and Byrnes, is one of the ten most frequent surnames in Ireland today. In the original Irish the name is *Ó Broin*, from the personal name *Bran*, meaning 'raven'. It is traced back to King Bran of Leinster, who ruled in the eleventh century.

As a result of the Norman invasion, the O'Byrnes were driven from their original homeland in Co. Kildare into south Co. Wicklow in the early thirteenth century. There they grew in importance over the years, retaining control of the territory until the early seventeenth century, despite repeated attempts by the English authorities to dislodge them.

Even today, the vast majority of the Irish who bear the name originate in Wicklow or the surrounding counties.

CAHILL

The original Irish from which the name derives is *Ó Cathail*, from the common personal name *Cathal*, sometimes anglicised 'Charles', which may in turn derive from the Old Irish *catu-ualos*, meaning 'strong in battle'.

Families of the name arose separately in different parts of Ireland, in Kerry, Galway, Tipperary and Clare. Originally the Galway family, located in the old diocese of Kilmacduagh near the Clare border, were most prominent, but their position was usurped by the O'Shaughnessys, and they declined. The southern families flourished, and the name is now most common in counties Cork, Kerry and Tipperary, while it is relatively infrequent in its other original homes. The arms illustrated are those of the Munster Cahills.

CARROLL

One of the twenty-five most common Irish surnames, Carroll comes, in the vast majority of cases, from the Irish *O Cearbhaill*, from *Cearbhall*, a very popular personal name thought to mean 'fierce in battle'. It is widespread today throughout Connacht, Leinster and Munster, reflecting the fact that it arose almost simultaneously as a separate surname in at least six different parts of Ireland.

The most famous of these were the Ely O'Carrolls of *Uíbh Fhailí*, including modern Co. Offaly as well as parts of Tipperary, who derived their name from *Cearball*, King of Ely, one of the leaders of the victorious native Irish army at the battle of Clontarf in 1014. Although their power was much reduced over the centuries in the continuing conflict with the Norman Butlers, they held on to their distinctive Gaelic way of life until the start of the seventeenth century.

CASEY

Casey, O'Casey and MacCasey come from the Irish *cathasach*, meaning 'vigilant in war', a personal name which was quite common in early Ireland. This, no doubt, accounts for the fact that *Ó Cathasaigh* arose as a separate surname in at least five distinct areas, in counties Cork, Dublin, Fermanagh, Limerick and Mayo, with *Mac Cathasaigh* confined to the Louth/Monaghan area. In medieval times, the Dublin and Fermanagh Caseys were the greatest and the most prominent, though their power, like that of other families, had been broken by the seventeenth century; the name is still common in north Co. Dublin to this day, as it is in Mayo and north Connacht generally. However, most present-day bearers of the surname are to be found in Munster, not only in Cork and Limerick, but also in Kerry and Tipperary.

CLANCY

The Irish version of the surname is *Mac Fhlannchaidh*, from the personal name *Flannchadh*, which, it is thought, meant 'red warrior'. It originated in two different areas, in counties Clare and Leitrim. In the former, where they were a branch of the McNamaras, their eponymous ancestor being *Flannchadh Mac Conmara*, the Clancys formed part of the great *Dál gCais* tribal group, and acted as lawyers, or 'brehons', to the O'Brien chieftains. Their homeland was in the barony of Corcomroe in north Clare, and they remained prominent among the Gaelic aristocracy until the collapse of that institution in the seventeenth century. The Leitrim family of the name were based in the Rosclogher area of the county, around Lough Melvin. Today, the surname is still common in Leitrim and Clare, with significant numbers also found in the adjacent counties.

CLEARY

Ó Cléirigh, meaning 'grandson of the scribe' is the Irish for both (O) Cle(a)ry and, in many cases in Ireland, Clarke, as outlined above. The surname is of great antiquity, deriving from *Cléireach* of Connacht, born c. 820. The first of his descendants to use his name as part of a fixed hereditary surname was *Tigherneach Ua Cléirigh*, lord of Aidhne in south Co. Galway, whose death is recorded in the year 916. It seems likely that this is the oldest true surname recorded anywhere in Europe. The power of the family in their original Co. Galway homeland was broken by the thirteenth century, and they scattered throughout the island, with the most prominent branches settling in Derry and Donegal, where they became famous as poets; in Cavan, where many appear to have anglicised the name as 'Clarke', and in the Kilkenny/Waterford/Tipperary region.

Castletown House, Co. Kildare, begun 1722 for a
member of the Connolly family.

CONNOLLY

A number of original Irish names have been anglicised as 'Connolly.' The *Ó Conghalaigh*, from *conghal*, 'as fierce as a wolf', were based in Connacht. The name arose as *Ó Coingheallaigh* in West Cork, while Ulster Connollys derive from both the *Ó Conghalaigh* of Fermanagh, and the Monaghan Connollys, for whom a number of separate origins are suggested, as a branch of the southern *Uí Néill*, or as a branch of the MacMahons. The latter Monaghan family has been the most prominent of the Connollys, recorded as having 'Chiefs of the Name' up to the seventeenth century, and producing, among others, Speaker William Conolly [sic], reputedly the richest man in eighteenth-century Ireland, and James Connolly, labour leader, socialist writer, and signatory of the 1916 Proclamation of Independence.

CROWLEY

In form Crowley is English, a habitation name from an Old English term meaning 'wood of the crows', and no doubt some of those in Ireland bearing the name derive from English stock. However, the vast majority are of Gaelic Irish extraction, with Crowley an anglicisation of *Ó Cruadhlaoich*, from *cruadh* and *laoch*, meaning 'hardy' and 'warrior'. The *Cruadhlaoch* from whom the family take their name was in fact one of the MacDermots of Moylurg in Connacht, who lived in the mid-11th century. Some time later, probably in the thirteenth century, some members of the family migrated from Connacht to Co. Cork, and their descendants prospered and multiplied while the original western branch of the family declined. The vast majority of Irish Crowleys today are connected to the Cork branch, and that county is still home to most of them.

CULLEN

The surname Cullen may be of Norman or Gaelic origin. The Norman name has been derived both from the city of Cologne in Germany, and from Colwyn in Wales. In Ireland this Norman family was prominent principally in Co. Wexford, where their seat was at Cullenstown castle in Bannow parish. Much more numerous in modern times, however, are descendants of the *Ó Cuilinn*, a name taken from *cuileann*, meaning 'holly-tree'. The name originated in southeast Leinster, and this area has remained their stronghold, with the majority to be found even today in counties Wicklow and Wexford. The most famous individual of the name was Paul Cullen (1803-78), Cardinal and Archbishop of Dublin, who presided over, and guided, the revival of the power of the Catholic Church in nineteenth-century Ireland.

DEMPSEY

In the original Irish Dempsey is *Ó Díomasaigh*, from *díomasach*, meaning 'proud'. The name was also occasionally anglicised 'Proudman'. The *Ó Díomasaigh* originated in the territory of Clanmalier, on the borders of what are now counties Laois and Offaly, and remained powerful in the area until the seventeenth century. James I recognised the strength of the family by granting the title 'Viscount Clanmalier' to Terence Dempsey. The loyalty of the family to the crown was short-lived, however, and the Williamite wars later in the century destroyed their power and scattered them. The surname is now found throughout the country. In Ulster, Dempsey is common in Co. Antrim, where it may be a version of 'Dempster', a Scottish name meaning 'judge', or possibly an anglicisation of *Mac Díomasaigh*, also sometimes rendered as 'McGimpsey'

18

DILLON

In Ireland Dillon may be of Gaelic or Norman origin, the former from *Ó Duilleáin*, possibly from *dall*, meaning 'blind', the latter from *de Leon*, from the place of the same name in Brittany. This, of course, accounts for the lion in the family arms. The Norman family have been prominent in Ireland since the arrival of their ancestor Sir Henry de Leon in 1185. He was granted vast estates in counties Longford and Westmeath, and his descendants retained their power up to modern times, with Co. Westmeath becoming known simply as 'Dillon's Country'. After the Williamite wars of the seventeenth century, a number of members of the family served in Continental armies. The best-known Irish regiment in the French army was 'Dillon's Regiment', many members of which made their way to America to fight against the British in the War of Independence.

DOHERTY

Doherty and its many variants – (O')Dogherty, Docherty, Dougharty etc., comes from the Irish *Ó Dochartaigh*, from *dochartach*, meaning 'unlucky' or 'hurtful'. The original *Dochartach,* from whom the clan descend, lived in the tenth century and has traditionally been claimed as twelfth in lineal descent from Conall Gulbain, son of Niall of the Nine Hostages, the fifth-century monarch supposedly responsible for kidnapping St Patrick to Ireland, and progenitor of the great tribal grouping of the *Uí Néill*. The original homeland of the O'Dohertys was in the barony of Raphoe in Co. Donegal, with the chief seat at Ardmire in the parish of Kilteevoge. They remained powerful chiefs in the area for five hundred years, until the defeat and execution of Sir Cahir O'Doherty in the the seventeenth century.

DONNELLY

Donnelly is *Ó Donnáile* in Irish, from Donnáil, a personal name made up of *donn*, meaning 'brown' and *gal*, meaning 'bravery'. The original ancestor was Donnáil O Neill, who died in 876, and was himself a descendant of Eoghan, son of Niall of the Nine Hostages, the fifth-century king who supposedly kidnapped St. Patrick to Ireland. Their territory was first in Co. Donegal, but they later moved eastwards into Co. Tyrone, where the centre of their power was at Ballydonnelly. Many of the family were hereditary bards, but their chief historical fame is as soldiers, especially in the wars of the seventeenth century. One modern bearer of the name who combined both traditional roles was Charles Donnelly (1910-37), poet and republican, who was killed fighting with the International Brigade in the Spanish Civil War.

DOWD

At the end of the nineteenth century, the vast majority of bearers of this surname were 'Dowd' rather than 'O'Dowd'. Since then, a large-scale resumption of the 'O' has reversed the proportions, with 'O'Dowd' now by far the most popular. The original Irish name was *Ó Dubhda*, from *dubh*, meaning 'black'. The family is one of the *Uí Fiachrach*, a large tribal grouping tracing its origin back to Fiachra, brother of Niall of the Nine Hostages, the fifth-century monarch supposedly responsible for kidnapping St Patrick to Ireland. The O'Dowds were the most powerful in this group, and their territory included large parts of northwest Mayo and west Sligo; the name is still numerous in the area today. The surname also rose in two other areas of the country: in Munster and in Derry, where the anglicisation is almost invariably 'Duddy'.

20

DUFFY

In Irish the surname is *Ó Dubhthaigh*, from *dubhthach*, meaning 'the dark one'. Several different families of the name arose separately in different places, the most important being in Donegal, Roscommon and Monaghan. In Donegal the family were centred on the parish of Templecrone, where they remained powerful churchmen for almost eight hundred years. The Roscommon family, too, had a long association with the church, producing a succession of distinguished abbots and bishops.

A Dublin bookseller.

DUNNE

Although 'Dunn' is also an English surname, from the Old English *dunn*, 'dark-coloured', the vast majority of those bearing the name in Ireland descend from the *Ó Doinn*, from *donn*, used to describe someone who was swarthy or brown-haired. The *Ó Doinn* first came to prominence as lords of the area around Tinnehinch in the north of the modern Co. Laois, and were known as Lords of Iregan up to the seventeenth century. At that time the surname was generally anglicised as 'O'Doyne'. Today the name is still extremely common in that part of Ireland, though it is now also widespread elsewhere. Perhaps because of the stronger English influence, in Ulster the name is generally spelt 'Dunn', while it is almost invariably 'Dunne' in other parts.

EGAN

Egan in Irish is *Mac Aodhagáin*, from a diminutive of the personal name *Aodh*, meaning 'fire', which was anglicised 'Hugh' for some strange reason. As well as Egan, *Aodh* is also the root of many other common Irish surnames, including O'Higgins, O'Hea, Hayes, McHugh, McCoy etc. The *MacAodhagáin* originated in the *Uí Máine* territory of south Roscommon/east Galway, where they were hereditary lawyers and judges to the ruling families. Over the centuries, however, they became dispersed southwards, settling mainly in north Munster and east Leinster. As well as Connacht, their original homeland, they are now most numerous in Leinster, though the surname is now also relatively widespread throughout Ireland. In both Connacht and Leinster the surname has also sometimes been anglicised as 'Keegan'.

FAHY

Fahy in Irish is *Ó Fathaigh*, probably from *fothadh* meaning 'base' or 'foundation'. Another, rarer, English version of the name is 'Vahey'. Strangely, it has also been anglicised as 'Green' because of a mistaken association with *faithce*, meaning 'lawn'. The name still has a very strong association with Co. Galway, where the historic homeland was situated. The area of the family's power was around the modern town of Loughrea in the south of the county, and the surname is still most plentiful in this area, despite the upheavals and migrations which have spread the name quite widely throughout Ireland. The best-known bearer of the name was Francis Arthur Fahy (1854-1935), songwriter and literary man, who paved the way for the Irish Literary Revival through his lifelong involvement with the Gaelic League and the London Irish Literary Society.

FARRELL

As both (O')Farrell and (O')Ferrall, this name in Irish is *Fearghail*, from the personal name *Fearghal*, made up of *fear*, 'man', and *gal*, 'valour'. The original *Fearghal* or Fergal from whom the family claim descent was killed at Clontarf in 1014. His great grandfather Angall gave his name to the territory they possessed, Annally in Co. Longford. The present name of both the county and the town derives from the family, the full name in Irish being *Longphuirt Uí Fhearghaíll*, O'Farrell's Fortress. They ruled this area for almost seven centuries, down to the final catastrophes of the seventeenth century, after which many members of the family fought with distinction in the armies of continental Europe. Today the surname is one of the most common in Ireland, with a wide distribution throughout the country, though the largest concentration remains in Longford.

FINNEGAN

In Irish the surname is *Ó Fionnagáin*, from *Fionnagán*, a diminutive of the popular personal name *Fionn*, meaning 'fairhaired'. It arose separately in two areas, on the borders of the present north Roscommon and north-east Galway, between the modern towns of Dunmore and Castlerea, and in the territory taking in parts of the present counties of Monaghan, Cavan and Louth. Descendants of the Connacht family are still to be found in the ancestral homeland, but the majority of modern Finnegans are descended from the Ulster family, and the name remains particularly numerous in counties Cavan and Monaghan. It is now also common throughout Ireland, with the exception of the southern province of Munster.

The ruins of the fourteenth-century Franciscan friary at
Askeaton, Co. Limerick.

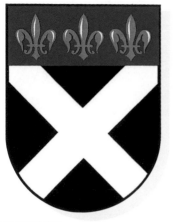

FITZPATRICK

Despite its Norman appearance, 'Fitz-' being Norman French for 'son of', in the vast majority of cases Fitzpatrick is an anglicisation of the Irish *Mac Giolla Phádraig*, meaning 'son of the servant of (St) Patrick'. Similarly to other surnames containing *Giolla*, it has also been anglicised as 'Kilpatrick' and, more rarely, 'Gilpatrick', principally in Ulster, where it is most common in counties Fermanagh and Monaghan. The original *Giolla Phádraig* from whom the surname is taken was the tenth-century ruler of the ancient kingdom of Upper Ossory, including parts of the present counties of Laois and Kilkenny. The surname was anglicised to Fitzpatrick in the early sixteenth century, when the chief of the family accepted the title of Lord Baron of Upper Ossory from Henry VIII. Partly due to this, they managed to retain possession of a large portion of their original lands up to the nineteenth century.

FLAHERTY

In Irish Flaherty and O'Flaherty are *Ó Flaithbheartach*, from *flaitheamh*, meaning 'prince' or 'ruler', and *beartach*, meaning 'acting' or 'behaving'. Although the literal translation is 'one who behaves like a prince', a more accurate rendition would be 'hospitable' or 'generous'. The family's original territory included the whole of the west of the modern Co. Galway, including Connemara and the Aran Islands, whence the title of their chief, Lord of Iar-Chonnacht and of Moycullen. They occupied and controlled this area from the thirteenth century on, and survived as a power in the area down to the eighteenth century. Although the name is now common and widespread, the largest numbers are still to be found in Co. Galway.

FLANAGAN

In Irish the surname is *Ó Flannagáin*, a diminutive of *flann*, a personal name which was very popular in early Ireland, and means 'red' or 'ruddy'. Perhaps because of this popularity, the surname arose separately in a number of distinct locations, including counties Roscommon, Fermanagh, Monaghan and Offaly. Of these, the most important families historically were those of Roscommon and Fermanagh. In the former location they were associated with the royal O'Connors, traditionally deriving from the same stock, and supplying stewards to the royal household. In Fermanagh they were rulers of territory covering the west of Lower Lough Erne, and based at Ballyflanagan, now the townland of Aghamore in Magheraboy parish. Today the surname is found throughout Ireland, though the largest concentration remains in southwest Ulster and north Connacht.

FLYNN

In Irish the name is *Ó Floinn*, from the adjective *flann*, meaning 'reddish', which was extremely popular as a personal name in early Ireland. As might be expected, this popularity led to the surname coming into being independently in several different parts of the country, including Clare, Cork, Kerry, Mayo, Roscommon, Cavan, Antrim and Monaghan. The most historically important of these were the families originating in Cork and Roscommon, with the former ruling over a territory in Muskerry between Ballyvourney and Blarney, and the latter centred on the area of north Roscommon around the modern town of Castlerea. In Co. Antrim the Irish version of the name was *Ó Fhloinn*, with the initial 'F' silent, so that the anglicised version became 'O'Lynn', or simply 'Lynn'. The O'Lynns ruled over the lands between Lough Neagh and the Irish Sea in south Antrim.

FOLEY

The original Irish for the surname is *Ó Foghladha*, from *foghlaidh*, meaning 'pirate' or 'marauder'. It originated in Co. Waterford, and from there spread to the nearby counties of Cork and Kerry. These are the three locations in which it is still most numerous, though it is now common throughout the southern half of the country. The best known modern Irish bearer of the name, Donal Foley (1922-81), journalist and humorist, came from the original homeland of Co. Waterford. The current Speaker of the U.S. House of Representatives is Congressman Tom Foley.

The desolate beauty of Glenmore Lake in Co. Kerry, now the stronghold of the Foleys.

FOX

Fox is an English surname, based on a nickname, and some Irish bearers of the name will be of English descent. In the majority of cases, however, Fox is a simple translation of *Ó* or *Mac an tSionnaigh*, 'descendant' or 'son of the fox' respectively. *Ó Sionnaigh* has a more particular history. Tadhg Ó Catharnaigh ('Kearney') was a chief in Co. Meath in the eleventh century and, for his wily ways, become known as '*An Sionnach*' the fox. As his descendants prospered, owning the entire barony of Kilcoursey in Co. Offaly and the title 'Barons Kilcoursey', they adopted his nickname as their surname, and the chief of the family took on 'The Fox' as a title. They lost their property after the rebellion of 1641-2, but the descent from the last Chief has remained unbroken. John William Fox, The Fox, Chief of his Name, recognised as such by the Chief Herald of Ireland, lives in Australia.

GALLAGHER

(O')Gallagher in Irish is *Ó Gallcobhar*, from *gall*, meaning 'foreign' and *cabhair*, meaning 'help' or 'support'. The original *Gallcobhar* from whom the family claim descent was himself descended from Conall Gulban, son of Niall of the Nine Hostages, the fifth-century monarch who was reputedly responsible for the kidnapping of St Patrick to Ireland, and the founder of the *Uí Néill* dynasty. The O'Gallaghers claim to be the most senior branch of the *Cinéal Conaill*, the group of families who all descend from Conall Gulban. Their territory was in *Tír Chonaill* (literally 'Conall's Land'), in what is now Co. Donegal. From the fourteenth to the sixteenth centuries they were hereditary commanders of the cavalry forces of the O'Donnell princes of *Tír Chonaill*. Today Gallagher is the single most numerous surname in Co. Donegal.

GORMAN

Gorman is a relatively common name in England, being derived from the Middle English name Gormund, from *gar*, meaning 'spear', and *mund*, meaning 'protection'. A few Irish Gormans may be of this connection, but in the majority of Irish cases the surname comes from the Irish *Mac Gormáin*, from a diminutive of *gorm*, meaning 'blue'. The original homeland was in Slievmargy, Co. Laois, but they were dispossessed by the Normans, and removed to counties Clare and Monaghan. The Clare branch became known for their wealth and for their patronage of poetry. From Clare they spread to Tipperary. When the native Irish began to resume the old O and Mac prefixes to their names in the nineteenth century, the Clare family mistakenly became 'O'Gorman'. In Tipperary, the name has mostly remained 'Gorman', while in Monaghan the original MacGorman still exists.

GRIFFIN

While the name is English in appearance, in the great majority of cases Irish Griffins are descended from the *Ó Gríobhtha*. Both the English and Irish versions ultimately have the same source, the name of the legendary monster, the gryphon, used as a nickname for someone fierce or dangerous. The name arose separately in at least two areas: in Co. Kerry, centred on Ballygriffin in Glanarought barony, and in Co. Clare, where the seat was at Ballygriffy, near Ennis. From these two starting points the families spread and intermingled, and today Griffin is among the 100 most common Irish surnames, found principally in the original homelands of Clare and Kerry, as well as in the adjoining counties of Cork and Limerick.

HEGARTY

In Irish the surname is *Ó hÉigceartaigh*, from *éigceartach*, meaning 'unjust'. The name appears to have arisen first in the area now divided between counties Derry and Donegal, where the *Ó hÉigceartaigh* were a branch of the Cinel Eoghain, a group of families claiming descent from Eoghan, one of the sons of Niall of the Nine Hostages, the fifth-century monarch who supposedly kidnapped St Patrick to Ireland. However, today the surname is much more common in Co. Cork, at the other end of the country. Traditionally, the Cork (O')Hegartys were claimed as a branch of the more historically prominent northern family, but *ecertach* was a common personal name in Munster, and it seems more likely that the surname arose separately there. At any rate, O'Hegartys are recorded in west Cork as early as the thirteenth century, and remain strongly associated with the area.

HENNESSY

The original Irish form of the name is *Ó hAonghasa*, from the personal name *Aonghas*, anglicised 'Angus', one of the pre-Christian Celtic gods. This was quite popular, and it gave rise to the surname in several distinct localities: in the north of the present Co. Offaly, from where the family later spread into the adjoining counties of Clare and Tipperary; in southwest Co. Cork, where they formed part of the *Corca Laoidhe* tribal grouping, descended from pre-Gaelic origins, and in east Cork, in the territory between Fermoy and Mitchelstown. The east Cork family produced the most famous bearer of the name, Richard Hennessy (1720-1800), who fought with Dillon's Brigade in the French army, and founded the famous brandy distillery in 1765. Today the surname is still associated with Co. Cork, though significant numbers also appear in counties Limerick, Tipperary and Clare.

HICKEY

The original Irish for Hickey is *Ó hIcidhe*, from *iceadh*, meaning 'healer'. The Hickeys were part of the tribal grouping, the *Dál gCais*, which produced Brian Boru, the High King of Ireland who defeated the Vikings in 1014. This grouping had its territory in the area now part of Co. Clare and north Tipperary, and it is this area with which the Hickeys remain closely identified. Their surname arose because of their position as hereditary physicians to the royal O'Brien family. From their original homeland, the name spread first into the neighbouring Co. Limerick, and from there even wider, so that Hickey is today one of the most common and widespread of Irish surnames.

HIGGINS

In form, Higgins is an English name, from the medieval name 'Higgin', a diminutive of 'Hicke', which was in turn a pet form of Richard. In Ireland, however, the majority of those bearing the name are of Gaelic Irish stock, Higgins being used as an anglicisation of the Irish *Ó hUigín*, from *uiginn*, meaning 'Viking'. The original *Uigín* from whom they claim descent was grandson to Niall of the Nine Hostages, the fifth-century king who founded the powerful tribal grouping the *Uí Néill*, and they are part of that grouping. Originally based in the midlands, they moved west over the centuries to Sligo and Mayo, and more than half of those bearing the surname today still live in the western province of Connacht. Don Ambrosio O'Higgins rose to become Viceroy of Peru for Spain, and his son, Bernardo, is widely remembered in South America as the 'Liberator of Chile'.

HOGAN

The Irish version of the surname is *Ó hÓgáin*, from a diminutive of *óg*, meaning 'young'. The original *Ógán* from whom the family claim descent lived in the tenth century and was an uncle of Brian Boru, the High King who defeated the Vikings at Clontarf in 1014. Like Brian Boru, they were part of the *Dál gCais* tribal grouping, whose original territory took in Clare and parts of Tipperary. The (O')Hogans were centred on Ardcrony, near the modern town of Nenagh in north Tipperary, where their chief had his seat. From there the surname spread far and wide, and is today one of the most common in Ireland, with particular concentrations close to the first homeland, in counties Clare, Tipperary and Limerick. In addition, significant numbers are to be found in Cork, where it is thought that the name may have had a separate origin, in the southwest of that county.

JOYCE

Joyce derives from the Breton name *Iodoc*, a diminutive of *iudh*, meaning 'lord', in Norman *Josse*. A number of English surnames arose from this, including Joyce, more often found in Ireland than anywhere else. The first bearer of the name in Ireland was a Thomas de Joise, of Norman Welsh extraction, who married a daughter of the O'Brien Princes of Thomond in 1283, and settled on the borders of the modern counties of Mayo and Galway. Their descendants became completely gaelicised, ruling that territory, still known as 'Joyce's Country', down to the seventeenth century. The surname remains associated with the area, with a large majority of Joyces originating in counties Galway and Mayo. The most famous modern bearer of the name was James Joyce (1882-1941), author of *Dubliners*, *Portrait of the Artist as a Young Man*, *Ulysses*, and *Finnegans Wake*.

KEANE

Like Kane, Keane is an anglicisation of *Ó Catháin*, from a diminutive of *cath*, meaning 'battle'. As an anglicisation, however, it is much more common in Connacht than in Ulster, the homeland of the Kanes. This is because *Ó Catháin* arose separately as a surname in Co. Galway, where the family were a branch of the historic *Uí Fiachra* tribal grouping. Traditionally it has been believed that the prominent Clare Keanes were an offshoot of the Ulster *Ó Catháin*, but the closeness of Clare and Galway must make this doubtful. A distinct family, the *Ó Céin* from Co. Waterford have anglicised their name as 'Kean', but without the final 'e'. The famous actors Edmund Kean (1787-1833) and his son Charles (1811-1880) were of this family.

KEARNEY

Kearney is widespread in Ireland, and has a number of different origins. In the west it originated in Co. Mayo, near Moynulla, the territory of the *Ó Cearnaigh* (from *cearnach*, meaning 'victorious'), where it has also been anglicised as Carney. A separate family of the same name, but anglicised as (O)Kearney, arose in Clare, and migrated in early times to the area around Cashel in Co. Tipperary. In Ulster the name derives from *Mac Cearnaigh*, also from *cearnach*; they were part of the *Cinéal Eoghain*, the large group of families descended from Eoghan, son of Niall of the Nine Hostages, the fifth-century monarch who founded the *Uí Néill* dynasty. The most historically important family, however, were the *Ó Catharnaigh*, from *catharnach*, meaning 'warlike'. These were chiefs of a large territory in the midlands, in the modern counties of Meath and Offaly.

KEATING

Although Keating is found as a surname in England, where it derives from the Old English *Cyting*, from *cyt*, meaning 'kite', in Ireland it is almost always of Norman origin. The family arrived with the Cambro-Norman invaders in the twelfth century and soon became thoroughly Irish, settling in south Leinster, and particularly in Co. Wexford, where the name is still very common. The most famous historical bearer of the name was Geoffrey Keating (or *Seathrún Céitinn*) the poet and historian who lived in the first half of the seventeenth century and wrote *Foras Feasa ar Éirinn,* a narrative history of the country defending it against the accounts given by foreign writers. In modern times the painter Seán Keating (1889-1977) specialised in traditional scenes, and was president of the Royal Hibernian Academy for fourteen years.

KELLY

Kelly comes from the Irish *Ó Ceallaigh*, based on Ceallach, which means either 'bright-haired' or 'troublesome'. The name was used as a surname in many places, including Co. Meath, the Antrim/Derry area, Galway/Roscommon and Co. Laois.

The greatest of these families are the O'Kellys of *Uí Máine*, or Hy Many, an old territory taking in east Galway and south Roscommon, also known simply as 'O'Kelly's Country'. They descend from Máine Mór, a fifth-century chief. A descendant was called Ceallach (died *c*.874) and the surname derives from him. His great-great-grandson Tadhg Mór, who died at the battle of Clontarf in 1014, was the first to use the name in an hereditary fashion. The succession to the position of head of the sept has remained unbroken: the present head is Walter Lionel O'Kelly of Gallagh and Tycooly, known as 'the O'Kelly'.

A brass seal in the shape of a monk,
bearing the O'Kelly arms.

John F. Kennedy (top right), and his family. Kennedy was
later to become the thirty-fifth president of the U.S.

KENNEDY

Kennedy in Irish is *Ó Cinnéide*, from a compound word meaning 'ugly-headed' or 'rough-headed'. The original bearer of the name, from whom the family claim descent, was a nephew of Brian Boru. His descendants were one of the most powerful families in the famous *Dál gCais* tribal grouping, and migrated from their homeland in Clare into adjoining north Tipperary, to become Lords of Ormond for over four hundred years up to the sixteenth century. From there the surname spread farther afield, becoming one of the most numerous in Ireland. In Ulster, many Kennedys are originally of Scottish stock, the MacKennedys being a branch of the Clan Cameron. The surname is now also common in Galloway and Ayrshire. The most famous modern bearer of the name was, of course, John F. Kennedy, president of the U.S., who was descended from a Wexford branch of the family.

KEOGH

Keogh, and its variant Kehoe, are the anglicisations of the Irish *Mac Eochaidh*, from *eoch*, meaning 'horse'. It arose as a surname in three distinct areas. The first was in south Roscommon, around Moyfinn in the barony of Athlone, which used to be known as 'Keogh's country'. This family was part of the *Uí Máine* tribal grouping. The second was in west Tipperary, near Limerick city; the place name Ballymackeogh marks the centre of their territory. The third and most important, both numerically and historically, was in Leinster, where the original homeland was in north Kildare, whence they migrated first to Wicklow and then south to Wexford. It is in Wexford that the name has been most commonly anglicised Kehoe. The surname is now most frequent in Leinster, though it has become widespread throughout Ireland.

LEARY

Leary and O'Leary derive from the original Irish *Ó Laoghaire*, from *Laoghaire*, meaning 'a keeper of calves'. Although there was a fifth-century king who gave his name to *Dún Laoghaire*, the port south of Dublin, no connection exists with the surname, which originated in Co. Cork and is even today to be found predominantly in that area. The family originally inhabited the rocky sea-coast of southwest Cork, between Roscarbery and Glandore, but the coming of the Normans displaced them, and they migrated to the mountains of Iveleary, which now incorporates their name, where they were and are particularly associated with the district of Inchigeelagh.

LYNCH

Lynch, which is today one of the most common surnames in Ireland, is unusual in that it has two completely distinct origins. The first is Norman, from *de Lench,* possibly derived from a place name now forgotten. The family settled initially in Co. Meath, and a branch then established itself in Galway, where they rapidly became one of the strongest of the 'Tribes of Galway'; one of their number, James Lynch, mayor in 1493, is reputed to have hanged his own son for murder when no one else could be found to carry out the sentence. The arms illustrated are for this family. The second origin for the name is Gaelic, from the Irish *Ó Loingsigh*, from *loingseach*, meaning 'seaman'. This arose in many areas, including Clare/Limerick, Sligo, west Cork, Cavan, Donegal and the north Antrim/Derry region, where they were chiefs of the old kingdom of *Dál Riada* in medieval times.

MACAULEY

MacAuley and its many variants – Cawley, Gawley, Macauley, Magawley etc. – may be either Scottish or Irish in origin. They are anglicisations of two distinct Irish surnames, *Mac Amhalgaidh* ('son of Auley') and *Mac Amhlaoibh* ('son of Auliff'). The former derives from a native personal name, and the family bearing the surname were rulers of a territory in what is now Offaly/Westmeath. The latter derives from a Gaelic version of the common Norse name 'Olaf', and the family claim descent from *Amhlaoibh,* son of the first Maguire king of Fermanagh, who ruled at the end of the thirteenth century. They gave their name to the barony of Clanawley in that county. An entirely distinct family, the MacAuliffs of Munster, are descended from Amhlaoibh MacCarthy. In Scotland also the surname and its variants have the same two distinct origins, from the Gaelic and Norse personal names.

MACCABE

MacCabe derives from the Irish *Mac Cába*, from *cába* meaning 'cape' or 'cloak'. The family are thought originally to have been a branch of the MacLeods of Harris in the Hebrides. They came to Ireland from there in the mid-fourteenth century to act as gallowglasses (mercenaries) to the O'Reillys and the O'Rourkes, the ruling families in the kingdom of Breffny, the territory now part of counties Longford and Cavan. They became completely hibernicized and adopted the customs and practices of the Irish, including internecine war; having established themselves in neighbouring Fermanagh by the fifteenth century, they continued the struggle for control with the Maguires up to the final catastrophe of the seventeenth century. The surname also became prominent in other adjoining counties, in particular Co. Monaghan.

MCCANN

There is dispute as to whether McCann comes from the Irish *Mac Anna*, 'son of Annadh', or *Mac Cana*, from *cana*, meaning 'wolf cub'. At any rate, the major family of the name were known as lords of Clanbrassil, an area on the southern shores of Lough Neagh in modern Co. Armagh, which they conquered from the O'Garveys. They appear to have been a branch of the *Cinéal Eoghain*, the group of families claiming descent from Eoghan, one of the sons of Niall of the Nine Hostages, the fifth-century founder of the *Uí Néill* dynasty. The death in 1155 of one of their chiefs, Amhlaoibh Mac Cana, is recorded in the Annals of the Four Masters with praise for his chivalry, his vigour, and the fine strong drink he made from the apples in his orchard. Today, the surname is found principally in counties Armagh, Tyrone and Antrim, though it has also spread to Leinster and Connacht.

MACCARTHY

MacCarthy comes from the Irish *Mac Cárthaigh*, from cárthach, meaning 'loving'. The Carthach from whom the surname is taken was king of Cashel c.1040, at a time when Donncha, son of Brian Boru, was king of Munster. Carthach was part of the dynasty claiming descent from Eoghan. The *Eoghanacht*, as they were known, had dominated Munster until the rise of Brian, part of the rival *Dál gCais*. The *Eoghanacht* resisted the *Dál gCais* fiercely, with the result that the MacCarthys and the O'Briens, with their respective allies, waged war for almost 150 years. In the twelfth century, the MacCarthys were expelled from their homeland in the Golden Vale in Co. Tipperary into the historic territory of Desmond, and it is with this area, which includes Cork and Kerry, that they have been most strongly associated ever since.

MACDERMOT

MacDermot comes from the Irish *Mac Diarmada*, from the personal name Diarmuid, which may derive from *dia*, 'god' and *armaid* 'of arms'. The individual from whom the surname is taken lived in the twelfth century, and was himself a descendant of Maolruanaidh Mór, brother of Conor, King of Connacht. Tradition has it that the two brothers came to an agreement that, in return for surrendering any claim to the kingship of Connacht, Maolruanaidh would receive Moylurg, an area in north Co. Roscommon. Certainly this is the area with which the descendants of Maolruanaidh, the MacDermots, have been closely associated ever since. For centuries their seat was a castle on MacDermot's Island, in Lough Key near Boyle.

Blarney Castle, owned by the MacCarthy family until the seventeenth century.

41

MACDONAGH

MacDonagh, and its many variants, MacDonough, Donogh, Donaghy etc., all derive from the Irish *Mac Donnchadha*, from *donnchadh* (often anglicised 'Donagh'), a popular first name meaning 'brown one'. The early popularity of the name meant that the surname based on it arose separately in two places: in Co. Cork, where the MacDonaghs were known as 'Lords of Duhallow', and in Co. Sligo, where the family were rulers in the barony of Tirreril. The Sligo MacDonaghs were in fact a branch of the MacDermotts, claiming Donagh MacDermott as their ancestor. Today the name is rare in Cork, but has become very widespread in the western province of Connacht. The best-known modern bearer of the name is Donagh MacDonagh (1912-1968), the poet, dramatist and lawyer, whose most successful play, *Happy as Larry*, has been translated into a dozen languages.

MACGILLYCUDDY

The surname comes from the Irish *Mac Giolla Mochuda*, meaning 'son of the devotee of (St) Mochuda'. Its adoption was unusual. St Mochuda, a pet form of Cárthach, meaning 'loving', was the seventh-century founder of the important monastic settlement of Lismore, in Co. Waterford. He was a native of Kerry, and when his fellow Kerryman Ailinn O'Sullivan became bishop of Lismore in the thirteenth century, he initiated the practice of the O'Sullivans paying particular devotion to this saint. As a result, the practice of using *Giolla Mochuda* as a kind of title grew among a leading family of the O'Sullivans . The first to use *Mac Giolla Mochuda* was Conor, who is recorded as having slain Donal O'Sullivan Beare in 1563. His family was known as 'MacGillycuddy O'Sullivan' or 'MacGillycuddy alias O'Sullivan' well into the seventeenth century, when MacGillycuddy became a surname in its own right.

MACMAHON

MacMahon (or MacMahon) comes from the Irish *Mac Mathghamha* or, in the modern version, *Mac Mathúna*, from *mathghamhqain*, meaning 'bear'. The surname arose separately in two areas, in west Clare and in Co. Monaghan. In the former, the MacMahons were part of the great tribal grouping, the *Dál gCais*, and claim decent from Mahon O'Brien, grandson of Brian Boru. The last Chief of the Name was killed at the battle of Kinsale in 1602. The Ulster MacMahons were based in the barony of Truagh in the north of Co. Monaghan, and ruled the kingdom of Oriel between the thirteenth and sixteenth centuries. Their last chief, Hugh MacMahon, was beheaded by the English in 1641. Today, although widespread throughout Ireland, MacMahon remains most common in the two ancestral homelands of Clare and Monaghan.

Ballymalis Castle stands in front of MacGillycuddy's Reeks, Co. Kerry.

MACNAMARA

MacNamara comes from the Irish *Mac Conmara*, 'son of the hound of the sea'. The surname arose in Co. Clare, where the family were part of the famous *Dál gCais* tribal grouping. They were second only to the O'Briens, to whom they were hereditary marshals. From fairly minor beginnings they became rulers of Clancullen, a territory including a large part of east Clare, where they held sway for almost six centuries, until the 1600s. Today, the surname is widespread throughout Ireland, but the largest concentration remains in the area of the original homeland, in counties Clare and Limerick. Brinsley MacNamara (1890-1963), the novelist and playwright, and the most famous modern bearer of the name, was in fact John Weldon. He used the pseudonym as protection; his most famous work, *The Valley of the Squinting Windows*, was very critical of Irish rural life.

MAGUIRE

Maguire comes from the Irish *Mag Uidhir*, meaning 'son of the brown(-haired) one'. The surname is very common throughout Ireland, with particular concentrations in Cavan, Monaghan and Fermanagh; in Fermanagh it is the single most numerous name in the county. The reason is not far to seek. From the time of their first firm establishment, all the associations of the family have been with Fermanagh. By the fourteenth century, the chief, Donn Carrach Maguire, was ruler of the entire county, and for the next 300 years there were no fewer than fifteen Maguire chieftains of the territory. By the year 1600, Co. Fermanagh quite simply belonged to the family.

Unlike the bulk of the native Irish aristocracy, the descent of the Maguires has remained intact. The current bearer of the title 'Maguire of Fermanagh' is Terence Maguire.

MALONE

Malone is the anglicised form of the Irish *Ó Maoil Eoin*, meaning 'descendant of a devotee of (St) John', *maol* being the Irish for 'bald' and referring to the distinctive tonsure sported by Irish monks. The family was an offshoot of the O'Connors of Connacht, and lived up to the ecclesiastical origin of their surname in their long connection with the famous Abbey of Clonmacnoise, with a long line of Malone bishops and abbots. Today they are largely dispersed from this area, and the greatest concentrations are to be found in counties Clare and Wexford. The most famous bearer of the name was Edmund Malone (1741-1812), a friend of Samuel Johnson, James Boswell, and Edmund Burke amongst others, whose complete edition of the works of Shakespeare remained standard for almost a century.

MORAN

Moran is the anglicisation of two distinct Irish names, *Ó Mórain*, from *mór*, meaning 'big', and *Ó Mughráin*, whose origins remain unclear. The former arose in Co. Mayo, near the modern town of Ballina, where the eponymous ancestor Móran held power. The latter family were part of the *UÍ Máine* tribal grouping. Their two branches were based around Criffon in Co. Galway, and the modern village of Ballintober in north Roscommon. Today, as might be expected, the vast majority of Morans are of Connacht origin. One of the most famous bearers of the name was Michael Moran (1794-1856), better known by his nickname of 'Zozimus', who was blinded in infancy and made his living on the streets of Dublin with his recitations and ballads. A monument to him stands in Glasnevin cemetery.

MORIARTY

Moriarty is the English version of the Irish *Ó Muircheartaigh*, made up of *muir*, 'sea', and *ceardach*, 'skilled', thus 'one skilled in the ways of the sea'. The name is undoubtedly linked to their original homeland, on both sides of Castlemaine harbour in south Co. Kerry. The continuity of their association with the area is remarkable, even by Irish standards. They have lived in the area since the surname came into being in the eleventh century, and ninety per cent of present births of the surname are still in Co. Kerry. This continuity is all the more tenacious for the fact that they had lost virtually all their power in the area by the fourteenth century. David Moriarty (1814-1877) was a Catholic bishop of Kerry notorious for his vehement denunciations of all opposition to the British government, saying of the Fenian leaders 'eternity is not long enough nor Hell hot enough for such miscreants.'

MURPHY

Murphy is the anglicised version of two Irish surnames, *Ó Murchadha* and *Mac Murchadha*, both derived from the Irish personal name *Murchadh*, meaning 'sea-warrior'. *Mac Murchadha* ('son of *Murchadh*') is exclusive to Ulster, where the family were part of the *Cinéal Eoghain*, the tribe descended from Eoghan, a son of the fifth century founder of the *Uí Néill* dynasty, Niall of the Nine Hostages. These Ulster Murphys (or MacMuphys) were originally based in Co. Tyrone, in the area known as *Muintir Birn*, but were driven out by the O'Neills and settled in south Armagh.

Elsewhere in Ireland, *O Murchadha* (descendant of *Murchadh*) is the original Irish. This arose separately in at least three areas: in Cork, Roscommon and Wexford. The greatest of these were the Wexford *Uí Murchadha*. These took their surname from *Murchadh* or Murrough, grandfather of Dermot MacMurrough, King of Leinster. Their territory lay in Ballaghkeen in Wexford, and was formerly known as Hy Felimy, from Felim, a son of Éanna Cinsealaigh, the fourth-century ruler of Leinster. During the onslaughts of the sixteenth century one branch of the family, based at Oularteigh, managed to retain their lands, and their succession continues unbroken to the present. David O'Morchoe (this version of the name was adopted by deed poll by his grandfather in 1895) is the current Chief of the Name. The arms illustrated are for this family.

The Murphys: 'even more Irish than those who are more Irish than the Irish!'

NOLAN

Nolan is now among the most common surnames in Ireland. It is the anglicised form of *Ó Nualláin*, from a diminutive of *nuall*, meaning 'famous' or 'noble'. The family are strongly linked with the area of the modern Co. Carlow, where in pre-Norman times they held power in the barony of Forth, whence their ancient title of 'Princes of Foharta'. Their power was greatly diminished after the arrival of the Normans, but the surname is still linked with the area. The prevalence of the surname in the modern counties of Mayo and Galway is explained by the migration of a branch of the family to that area in the sixteenth century; they obtained large tracts of land, and their descendants are many. The most famous modern bearer of the surname was the writer Brian O'Nolan (1911-1966), better known under his two pen-names of Flann O'Brien and Myles na Gopaleen.

O'BRIEN

O'Brien is in Irish *Ó Briain*, from the personal name Brian. The meaning of this is problematic. It may come from *bran*, meaning 'raven', or, more likely, from *Brion*, a borrowing from the Celtic ancestor of Welsh which contains the element *bre*, meaning 'hill' or 'high place'. By association, the name would then mean 'lofty' or 'eminent'. The surname itself denotes a descendant of the great Brian Boru, ('Brian of the Tributes'), High King of Ireland and victor at the battle of Clontarf in 1014. He secured submission from all tribes but the northern *Uí Néill*, the Leinstermen and the Vikings, and his victory at Clontarf united all of Ireland, nominally at least, under a single leader, though Brian himself was slain. The family spilt into a number of branches, including the O'Briens of Aherlow, the O'Briens of Waterford and the O'Briens of Limerick.

The Cliffs of Moher, Co. Clare, the original home of the mighty Brian Boru.

O'CALLAGHAN

O'Callaghan comes from the Irish Ó *Ceallacháin*, from the personal name Ceallachán, a diminutive of *ceallach*, thought to mean 'bright-headed'. The personal name was favoured by the *Eoghanacht*, the tribes who controlled the kingship of Munster; it is from one of the *Eoghanacht* kings, Ceallachán (d.954), that the family trace their descent. By the end of the thirteenth century the O'Callaghans had taken possession of a large area around the River Blackwater west of Mallow, Co. Cork, which came to be known as O'Callaghan's Country. Here they held sway for four centuries, keeping many of the earlier Gaelic customs. The most notorious of these was the cattle-raid; one chief of the family was said to have led two hundred raids in Munster. In the seventeenth century the family lost everything: the chief, Donncha O'Callaghan, and his extended family were transplanted to east Clare.

O'DONOVAN

O'Donovan comes from the Irish Ó*Donndubháin*, from *donn*, 'brown' and *dubh*, "dark', the surname meaning 'descendant of the dark brown (-haired/complexioned) man'. The Donnduban from whom the surname derives was king of *Uí Chairpre* in east Limerick, and died in 980. In the twelfth century, as a result of the struggle between the MacCarthys and the O'Briens for Munster, the O'Donovans were forced to migrate to Cork. There they gave the name of their kingdom to the modern barony of Carbery. The family remained powerful into the seventeenth century, when, like so many members of the native aristocracy, the chiefs of the family were dispossessed in punitive confiscations. They managed to regain some property in the area after the Treaty of Limerick, however, and re-established the family seat at Bawnlahan in the parishes of Myross and Castlehaven.

Co. Kerry. Love of the land is an intensely Irish
characteristic – and the land is easy to love.

O'HARA

O'Hara is a phonetic anglicisation of *Ó hEaghra*. The family claim descent from *Eaghra*, lord of Luighne (the modern Leyney) in Co. Sligo, who died in 976 and who was himself, in the traditional genealogies, of the family of Oiloll Ollum, king of Munster. The O'Haras remain strongly associated with Co. Sligo, where they were chiefs in two areas, *Ó hEaghra Buidhe* ('fair') around Collooney, and *Ó hEaghra Riabhach* ('grey') at Ballyharry, more properly 'Ballyhara'. In the fourteenth century a branch of the family migrated north to the Glens of Antrim and established themselves in the area around the modern town of Ballymena. There they intermarried with powerful local families and acquired great prominence themselves. Apart from Dublin, Sligo and Antrim are still the two regions where the surname is most concentrated.

O'KEEFFE

O'Keeffe, and Keeffe, are the anglicised versions of the Irish *Ó Caoimh*, from *caomh*, meaning 'kind' or 'gentle'. The original *Caomh* from whom the family descend lived in the early eleventh century, and was a descendant of Art, King of Munster from 742 to 762. Originally the territory of the family lay along the banks of the Blackwater river in Cork, but the arrival of the Normans displaced them, like so many others, and they moved west into the barony of Duhallow, where their territory became known, and is still known, as Pobal O'Keeffe. The chiefs of the family retained power down to the eighteenth century, despite their involvement in the various rebellions, but were eventually dispossessed. Even today, Pobal O'Keeffe is still the area in which the name is most common, with surrounding areas of Co. Cork also including many of the name. It remains relatively rare outside that county.

O'MAHONY

O'Mahony, the most common contemporary form of the name, comes from the Irish *Ó Mathghamhna*, stemming from *mathghamhan*, meaning 'bear'. The surname was adopted in the eleventh century by one of the dominant families of the Munster *Eoghanacht* peoples, the *Cinéal Aodha*. With the rise of the MacCarthys in the twelfth century the influence of the O'Mahonys was largely confined to the two areas of Cork with which they are still most strongly associated, the Iveagh peninsula and the barony of Kinalmeaky, around Bandon. In these areas they retained power until the wars of the seventeenth century. The most famous modern bearer of the name was Eoin ('the Pope') O'Mahony (1904-1970), barrister and genealogist, who preserved with enthusiasm the traditions of his own and many other families, organizing the annual clan gathering of the O'Mahonys.

O'ROURKE

O'Rourke comes from the Irish *Ó Ruairc,* from a name derived from the Old Norse *Hrothekr* meaning 'famous king'. The Ruarc from whom the surname derives was a ninth-century king of Breifne, an area covering most of Leitrim and Cavan. The first to use his name as an hereditary surname was his grandson, Seán Fearghal Ó Ruairc. Over the next 150 years, four O'Rourkes were Kings of Connacht. After the twelfth century, they submitted to the overlordship of the O'Connors, and also had problems with the other great family of Breifne, the O'Reillys, which ultimately resulted in their territory shrinking. The family stronghold was at Dromahair in Co. Leitrim. The line of descent from the last Chief of the Name, Brian Ballagh O'Rourke, who was inaugurated in 1529, remains intact. The present holder of the title 'O Ruairc of Breifne' is Philip O Rorke, resident in London.

O'SHEA

O'Shea, Shea and (O')Shee are anglicisations of the Irish *Ó Séaghdha*, from the personal name *Séaghdha*, meaning either 'hawk-like' or 'fortunate'. The surname arose in south Kerry, on the Iveragh peninsula, where the family held power in the early Middle Ages. Despite the later decline in their influence, they were not displaced, remaining extremely numerous in their original homeland down to the present day. The surname is also found in some numbers in counties Tipperary and Kilkenny. These are the descendants of family members who migrated north as early as the fourteenth century. They became prominent in Kilkenny especially, where the name was more often anglicised (O')Shee. The most famous bearer of the name in Irish history was Katharine O'Shea, mistress and later wife of Charles Stewart Parnell; their love affair brought about Parnell's downfall and changed the course of Irish history.

The falls at Glen Macnass, near Laragh in Co. Wicklow.

POWER

Power is originally a Norman name, which may derive from the Old French *povre*, meaning 'poor', or from *pohier*, meaning a native of the town of *Pois* in Picardy in France, so called from the Old French *pois*, meaning 'fish', a name given it because of its rivers. The surname is also found in Ireland as 'Le Poer', and in the Irish version 'de Paor'. The first Norman settlers of the name were in Co. Waterford, where members of the family retained large estates up to the nineteenth century, and the surname is still most numerous by far in that county, although it has also spread into the adjoining counties of Kilkenny, Cork, Tipperary and Wexford. The family which founded Power's distillery, famous for its whiskey, were from Wexford, with their seat at Edermine, near Enniscorthy.

QUIGLEY

Quigley is the principal English version of the Irish *O Coigligh*, from *coigleach*, meaning 'unkempt'. The main origin of the family was in in Co. Mayo, where they were part of the powerful *Uí Fiachrach* tribal grouping. From there they were dispersed at an early date, principally to the adjacent territories now part of counties Sligo, Donegal and Derry, where the name is principally found today. There appears also to have been a separate *Ó Coigligh* family which arose in Co. Wexford, where the name has been anglicised for the most part as 'Cogley', although Quigley is also frequent.

QUINN

Quinn is now among the twenty most common Irish surnames in the country. The name arose separately in four areas. In three of these – near Corofin in Co. Clare, in the glens of north Antrim, and in Co. Longford – the Irish original from which the surname derives is *Ó Coinn*, from *Conn*, a personal name meaning 'chief' or 'leader'. The most notable of these families is that based in Clare, where the barony of Inchiquin bears their name; in early times they were chiefs of the Clan Heffernan, and their descendants are today Earls of Dunraven and Mountearl. The fourth area is Tyrone, where the surname is the most common in the county. Here the descent is claimed from *Coinne*, a great-great-grandson of Niall of the Nine Hostages, the fifth-century monarch who founded the dynasty of the *Uí Néill*. In the fighting forces of the O'Neills, the *Ó Coinne* were traditionally quartermasters.

REGAN

Regan, along with its variants Reagan and O'Re(a)gan, comes from the Irish *Ó Ríagáin*, perhaps from *ríodhgach*, meaning 'impulsive' or 'angry'. It originated in at least three different areas. In the Meath/Dublin region it was borne by one of the Four Tribes of Tara, who migrated to Co. Laois, where their descendants are still to be found. A second family claims descent from Riagán, a nephew of the eleventh-century High King Brian Boru; their homeland was the kingdom of Thomond, in Co. Limerick. East Cork, around Fermoy, was the original territory of the third family of *Ó Riagáin*. Their influence in the area of east Cork is recorded in the townland names of Coolyregan and two Ballyregans. By the sixteenth century most members of this family had migrated to the southwest, however, and it is with west Cork that the name is most strongly linked today.

REILLY

Reilly, with its variants Riley and (O')R(e)ily, comes from the Irish *Ó Raghallaigh*, and is extremely common and widespread throughout Ireland. It originated in the old kingdom of Breffny, which included areas now in counties Cavan and Longford, where the O'Reillys were long the dominant family. Their prosperity may be gauged by the fact the 'reilly' was at one point a colloquial term for money in Ireland. After the collapse of Gaelic power in the seventeenth century large numbers emigrated to serve in the armies of France, many in Colonel Edmund O'Reilly's regiment of foot. The connection with the original homeland is still strong, however; even today (O')Reilly is the single most numerous surname in both Cavan and Longford.

RIORDAN

Riordan, with its variants O'Riordan and Reardan, comes from the Irish original *Ó Rioghbhárdáin* (*Ó Ríordáin* in modern Irish), *riogh-* meaning 'royal', and *bárdán* a diminutive of *bard*, 'poet'. The surname originated in the area between the modern towns of Thurles in Co. Tipperary and Birr in Co. Offaly. Very early, perhaps even in the twelfth century, the *Ó Rioghbhárdáin* migrated south to Co. Cork, where they settled in the west of the county, in Muskerry particularly, and the strength of their association with this part of the country remains remarkable; a large majority of those bearing the name originate in Co. Cork. Seán Ó Riordáin (1916-1971), born in Ballyvourney, Co. Cork, is considered by many to have been the finest Irish-language poet of the twentieth century.

ROCHE

Roche is a name of Norman origin. Although the obvious derivation is from the French *roche*, 'rock', the earliest bearer of the surname in Ireland, Richard FitzGodebert de la Roche, in fact adopted the surname after his place of origin in Wales, Rhos in Pembrokeshire. He was one of the first Norman arrivals, coming in 1167, and acquiring large tracts of south Co. Wexford. Over the centuries the family became thoroughly hibernicized, to the point where they were prominent in the many rebellions against English rule, the best-known being Father Philip Roche, who led the Irish in the Battle of Horetown in 1798. The name is still strongly linked with Co. Wexford, where a townland of Rochestown exists today, but over the centuries many of the family migrated south, particularly to the area around the modern town of Fermoy in Co. Cork, where they prospered greatly.

RYAN

Ryan is today one of the commonest surnames in Ireland. Unlike many other common surnames, however, it has one major origin, in the family of *Ó Maoilriaghain*, meaning 'descendant of a devotee of St Riaghan'. The anglicisation 'Mulryan' began to fade as early as the seventeenth century, and is today virtually unknown. The surname first appears in the fourteenth century in the barony of Owney, on the borders of counties Limerick and Tipperary, where the *Ó Maoilriaghain* displaced the O'Heffernans. Even today the surname is highly concentrated in this area. In Carlow and adjoining areas Ryan may also derive from *Ó Riaghain*, sometimes confused with Regan. Patrick J. Ryan (1883-1964) emigrated to the U.S., won a gold medal for hammer-throwing for that country in the 1920 Olympics, and then returned to farming in Pallasgreen in Limerick.

SHEEHAN

Sheehan is the anglicisation of the Irish *Ó Síodhacháin*, from a diminutive of *síodhach*, meaning 'peaceful'. The principal family of the name were part of the *Dál gCais*, the tribal grouping occupying an area in Limerick and Clare which produced Brian Boru, High King of Ireland, in the eleventh century. Some of the traditional genealogies have the descent of the Sheehans from one Sidhechan, a contemporary of Brian Boru and distantly related to him. Initially they appear to have lived in the south of Co. Limerick, in the barony of Connello. In very early times, however, they migrated south, into the northeast of the present Co. Cork, where they are still most numerous. Over the course of the centuries, large numbers have also migrated into Co. Kerry, while a significant number also remained in their homeland of Limerick. In these areas, the surname is very common indeed.

SHERIDAN

Sheridan is the English version of *Ó Sirideáin*, from the personal name *Sirideán*, which is possibly related to *sirigh*, 'to seek'. The surname arose in the modern Co. Longford, where the *Ó Sirideáin* held hereditary church offices and land in the parish of Granard. They later moved to the adjoining county of Cavan, where they became followers of the rulers of Breffny, the O'Reillys. Cavan is still the area in which the surname is most common, though it has now spread throughout the northern half of the country. The most famous bearer of the name was the playwright Richard Brinsley Sheridan (1751-1817), born in Dublin, whose three masterpieces, *The Rivals*, *The School for Scandal* and *The Critic* display brilliant comic invention.

SWEENEY

Sweeney comes from the Irish *Mac Suibhne*, from *suibhne*, meaning 'pleasant'. The original *Suibhne* from whom the surname derives was a Scottish chief based in Argyle around the year 1200. His people were of mixed Viking and Irish descent, and their fame as fighters meant that they were much in demand as mercenaries. Suibhne's great-great-grandson Muchadh Maer Mac Suibhne settled in Co. Donegal in the fourteenth century, and his offspring soon split into distinct groups, the principal ones being *Mac Suibhne Fanad* and *Mac Suibhne na dTuath*. Up to the final defeat of the seventeenth century, they fought as mercenaries in the struggles of Ulster. Members of both groups also made their way to Cork in the fifteenth century, acquiring territory in Muskerry. The Cork family prospered, and today the surname is more numerous in the Cork area than in Ulster.

TOBIN

Tobin is in Irish *Tóibín*, which is a Gaelicised version of the Norman 'St Aubin', after the place of the same name in Brittany, so called from the dedication of its church to St Albin. The family came to Ireland in the immediate aftermath of the Norman invasion, and by the early thirteenth century were well established in counties Kilkenny and Tipperary; their power in the latter county is attested by the (unofficial) title 'Baron of Coursey', by which the head of the family was known in the Middle Ages. In the course of time the surname also spread into the adjoining counties of Cork and Waterford, and this is the area in which it remains most common by far today. The two best-known contemporary bearers of the name in Ireland are the comic actor Niall Tóibín and the novelist and poet Colm Tóibín.

WALSH

Walsh is among the five most numerous surnames in Ireland, with particular concentrations in counties Mayo and Galway, in Munster in counties Cork and Waterford, and in Leinster in counties Kilkenny and Wexford. It is a semi-translation of the Irish surname *Breathnach*, meaning 'British' or 'Welsh', also sometimes anglicised as 'Brannagh'. Unlike most of the other Hiberno-Norman families who can trace their ancestry to a small number of individuals, the Walshes have many origins, since the name arose independently in different places, for obvious reasons. Two exceptions should perhaps be mentioned: the descendants of Haylen Brenach, one of those who arrived in 1172, became very well known and prosperous in the south and east of the country, while 'Walynus', who arrived in 1169, is said to have been the progenitor of the Walshes of Tirawley in Co. Mayo.

WHELAN

Whelan, along with its common variant Phelan, comes from the Irish *Ó Faoláin*, from a diminutive of *faol*, 'wolf'. Taken together, the two names come among the fifty most numerous in Ireland. The family originated in the ancient kingdom of Decies, part of the modern county of Waterford, where they were rulers up to the Norman invasion. From this centre the surname has now spread to the adjoining counties of Kilkenny, Cork, Wexford and, further north, Carlow. It is also to be found throughout the country, however. The best known modern bearer of the name was Seán Ó Faoláin, the novelist and short-story writer, whose writing career spanned six decades. His family name was originally Whelan. His daughter Julia is also a distinguished novelist.